P♥RN FOR THE
Working WOMAN

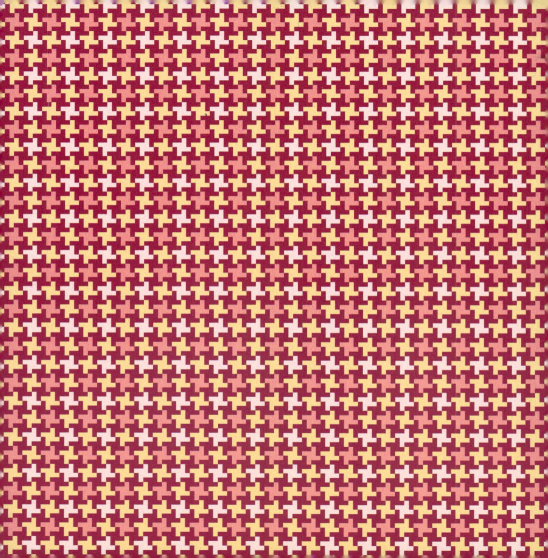

PORN FOR THE Working WOMAN

From the Cambridge Women's Pornography Cooperative

Photographs by Gretchen LeMaistre

CHRONICLE BOOKS

SAN FRANCISCO

A PORN FOR book.
PORN FOR is a trademark of Urgent Haircut Productions.

Library of Congress Cataloging-in-Publication Data available.
ISBN: 978-1-4521-2139-0

Manufactured in China

Photography Assistant: Kirk Crippens
Wardrobe/Props: Georgie Perrins
Stylist Assistant/Props: Christiana Coop
Models: Ashkon, Bill, Chip, Joe, Oracio and Oz

10 9 8 7 6 5 4 3 2

Chronicle Books LLC
680 Second Street
San Francisco, California 94107
www.chroniclebooks.com

What do women *really* want in the workplace?

Opportunity. Advancement based on merit. Respect for our ideas and opinions. Equal pay. Blah, blah, blah. . . . ***Of course we want that stuff!*** But what would make work more ***delightful?*** That's the question the Cambridge Women's Pornography Cooperative set out to answer with *Porn for the Working Woman*.

As with our previous research projects,

Porn for Women, Porn for Moms, Porn for Women of a Certain Age, and others, we're reclaiming the term porn, and using it to incorporate fantasies in every corner of our busy lives.

So at our workplace, there are yoga breaks, company pedicurists, afternoon dessert carts, dream assignments from the boss, and clear rules for guys about toilet seat etiquette!

Enjoy!

Oh, I didn't expect you
back from lunch so soon.
*I haven't even changed
your flowers yet.*

We're done with these Manolo Blahnik samples for the photo shoot. Looks like they're *all your size . . .*

The big client dinner got canceled tonight. But look, since we already paid a fortune for the chef and private dining room, *why don't you and some friends* go and use it.

Don't worry about a thing while you're at work today, Honey.

I don't know why we even bother doing your review. *You're fabulous.*

Look, I know I'm just a man, but I can *do* the job. *Just give me a chance* to prove it.

COMPANY POLICY
$500 FINE
For Leaving Seat UP
$1,000 FINE
For Peeing with Seat DOWN

Wow. Who would've guessed that *team-building shopping* would be so much fun?

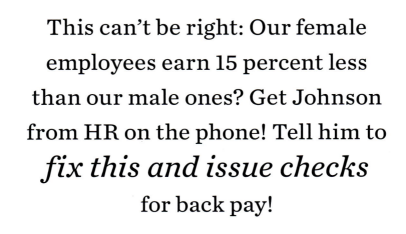

This can't be right: Our female employees earn 15 percent less than our male ones? Get Johnson from HR on the phone! Tell him to *fix this and issue checks* for back pay!

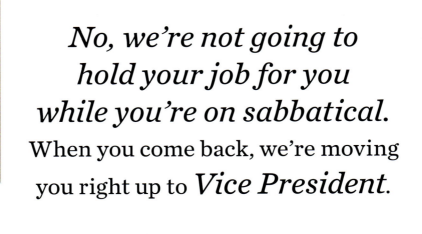

No, we're not going to hold your job for you while you're on sabbatical. When you come back, we're moving you right up to *Vice President.*

Hi, Sweetie. You know that accounting lunch-meeting on your schedule? It's actually me. *I booked us a table at your favorite restaurant*, and I can't wait to see you.

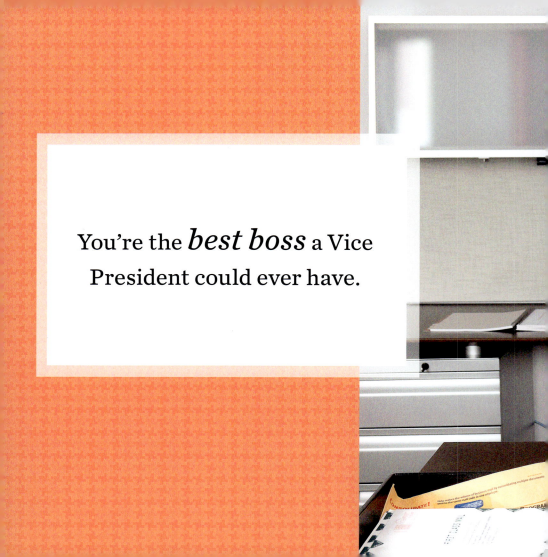

You're the *best boss* a Vice President could ever have.

I'm sick of Casual Fridays. From now on, we're having Casual Mondays through Fridays!

Anything from the *afternoon dessert cart* today?

Hi, I'm your dedicated coffee boy, Steve.

Text me your order anytime, and it'll be on your desk in five minutes.

Your presentation blew me away. *Take the rest of the day off.*

I love that they bring in guest chefs for us during the workday!

Would you be willing to consider running the Rome office this summer? It comes with a residence, a nanny, a stipend so you can bring the family, and, of course, a cash bonus.

Good call skipping the lame-o office birthday party for Ronald. But I figured *that's no reason to miss a great piece of cake.*

These things are ridiculous! From now on, *dress code is flats only.*

Am I the *only one* around here who *cares* if we have a clean break room?

Got the dry cleaning, upgraded your plane tickets, and I'll stay home to meet the plumber tomorrow. *Anything else I can do?*

"Yoga break!"

I'd like to pitch this spa
client next week.
Would you be willing to go
*check it out for a
couple of days?*

If I work hard, someday I'll be
in charge, and have the
big office . . . like *she* has.

The boss wants you upgraded: *first class air, suite at the hotel, and two massage vouchers.*

I will talk to women's faces, not to
I will talk to women's faces, not to
I will talk to women's faces, not to
will talk to women's faces, not to
talk to women's faces, not to
talk to women's faces, not to
talk to women's faces, not to
talk to women's faces, not to
talk to faces, not to
talk to faces, not to
Talk faces, not to
talk to women's faces,
to their boobs
talk to women's faces,
to their boobs
will talk to women's faces,
to their boobs
will talk to women's faces,
to their boobs
I will talk to women's faces,
not to their boobs
I will talk to women's faces,
not to their boobs
I will talk to women's faces,
not to their boobs
I will talk to women's faces,
not to their boobs

Don't even worry about it.
I'll just order you a new one.

How big do you want the window in your new *corner office?*

I'm the *company pedicurist.*
Want me to work under your desk
while you take your conference call?

Your office comes with your choice of furnishings, *a separate sitting room, and a private bath.*

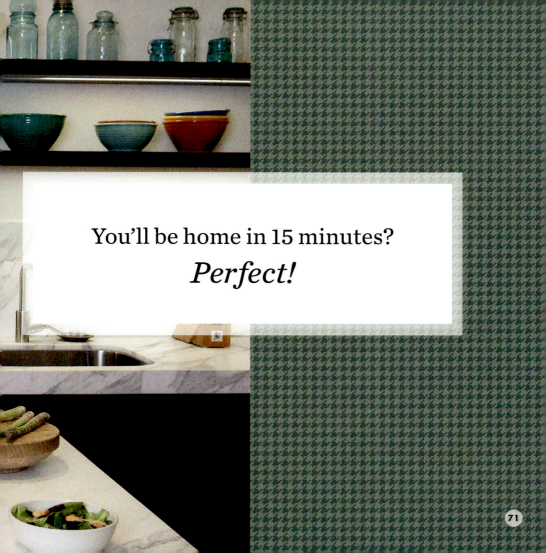

You'll be home in 15 minutes?
Perfect!

Office **Porn** Pop Quiz

You're excited about something your kid did last night. You come in and tell your colleague about it. Does he

A   turn away from his computer, ask for all the details, and then shout to other colleagues that they've got to hear about this amazing kid?

B   nod politely, and say he remembers when his kid was at that stage.

C   say, "Finally, a little pay off for all those extra kid-bearing pounds."

You have to leave early to pick up your kid, who's not feeling well at school. Does your boss say,

A   "Go right away. I'll finish the stuff you're working on."

B   "Well, okay, but would you mind finishing up your work tonight so we don't get behind on anything?"

C   "Collateral damage from another one of your dinners, huh?"

It's your birthday. What happens at work?

A   Your boss and colleagues all take you out to a nice, long lunch at your favorite restaurant and sing your praises.

B   Your colleagues all get together for the obligatory singing of "Happy Birthday" around a supermarket cake.

C   Your boss walks by, pops his head in and says, "Hey, move a little faster on that project, will ya? As of today, you're a year closer to our mandatory retirement age."

The owner of your company's biggest client is coming to town. What does your boss say to you?

A   "You know this guy better than I do. You handle all the plans—and don't worry about the budget."

B   "I think I'd better take the lead on this. This is our biggest client, after all."

C   "Hey, think you could take his wife shopping?"

You arrive a few minutes late because it was your turn to do the carpool one morning. Does your colleague say,

A   "Here she is: employee of the year and supermom!"

B   "Don't worry, I've been late too, at times. But it's usually because I'm hungover."

C   "I'd be late, too, if I had to cram that body into those pants."

You make a presentation that you've been working on for weeks. Right after you're done, the boss walks up and says,

A "That was amazing. No one else in the company could have done that. I'm in awe of your talents."

B "Not bad. Let's get back to work."

C "Who was that model you used in the third slide? Does she work here?"

You work in a cubicle, and a nice office with a window opens up. You're clearly the next in line to get it. What does your boss say?

A "Have a look at the furnishings, and let me know what we should change. I'd like it to reflect your good taste when you move in."

B "Well, it's your turn."

C "Now when you have PMS, we can just bolt the door."

You walk into the office lunchroom to get your food out of the fridge. What happens?

A You see a beautiful spread of food, and your boss says, "Surprise! I thought you guys deserved a really special meal today."

B You get your lunch out of the fridge, but you noticed that someone has filched your brownie again.

C You open the fridge, the smell overwhelms you, and through teary, burning eyes, you see something green and fuzzy growing on your lunch bag.

You feel like dressing up for work, so you put on a dress and a pair of heels. What does your cubicle-mate say when you arrive?

A   "Wow, you look great. Special occasion, or just feel like wowing us?"

B   "Job interview?"

C   "Working nights, are we?"

Your boss receives a call that his wife has broken her ankle, and is in the emergency room. What does he say to you as he's heading out the door?

A   "Thank goodness you're here. It's such a relief to know this place will be in great hands while I'm gone."

B   "I hope to be back tomorrow. Don't leave early!"

C   "Hey, looks like she's going to be in the hospital overnight. You busy?

PORN POINTS

A = 3 points
B = 1 point
C = -3 points

15–30: **Boss of the year!**
1–15:   **Have your boss read this book. Twice.**
-30–0: **Hopeless! Seek an immediate boss upgrade.**

What makes you hot?

Finding out **what women really want**, and getting that information into the public domain, has been the life's work of the Cambridge Women's Pornography Cooperative. Please help support our important scientific breakthroughs by sharing these findings with friends, neighbors, and colleagues.

Go to our website, www.wannasnuggle.com,
to see and e-mail, results from the original *Porn for Women* and *XXX Porn for Women: Hotter, Hunkier, and more Helpful around the House!,* as well as our groundbreaking *Porn for New Moms.*

Were you **inspired by these photos** to come up with a *Porn for Women* scenario of your own? Send it to us. We may include it in a future study, and maybe it'll even get published someday. That'll make you an honorary member of the Cambridge Women's Pornography Cooperative.